THE STORY OF
MONEY

JOHN ORNA-ORNSTEIN

Published for the Trustees of the British Museum
by British Museum Press

To Katy

Acknowledgements

Thanks firstly to Joe Cribb, whose advice, knowledge and support were essential to
every stage of the production of this book. Special thanks, too, to Carolyn Jones and
Janet Larkin for their constant hard work and patience.
I am grateful to all of the staff of the Department of Coins and Medals, British Museum
Press (especially Catherine Wood), The British Museum Photographic Service (principally
Jeff Hopson), and the other British Museum departments who helped in preparing and
publishing this book.

The Trustees of the British Museum acknowledge with gratitude generous assistance
towards the HSBC Money Gallery and the production of this book from

HSBC Holdings plc

Consultant: Joe Cribb, Curator of the HSBC Money Gallery, Department of Coins and
Medals, British Museum

First published in 1997 by
British Museum Press
A division of The British Museum Company
46 Bloomsbury Street, London WC1B 3QQ

A catalogue record for this book is available from the British Library

ISBN 0 7141 0884 7

Original artwork by Bruce Hogarth/David Lewis Associates
Designed by Peartree Design Associates
Cover design Slatter Anderson Associates
Printed in Slovenia by Korotan

CONTENTS

Money   4

Coins   6

Paper money   8

Salt, stones and plastic   10

The earliest money   12

The ancient Greeks   14

The Romans   16

The Middle Ages   18

The Renaissance   20

Asia   22

Islam   24

Africa   26

The Americas   28

Money talks   30

Coins and the archaeologist   32

Past and present   34

Forgery   36

Hoarding   38

The magic of money   40

Gifts   42

Fascinating facts   44

Collecting and learning   46

Index and Further reading   48

MONEY

This book looks at the story of money, a story that began thousands of years ago and that affects every country in the world. Today, nearly everyone uses money. Without it we could not buy food or clothes or pay bills. Many different kinds of money have been used in the past. Looking at all these types of money is a fascinating way of learning about far-away times and places.

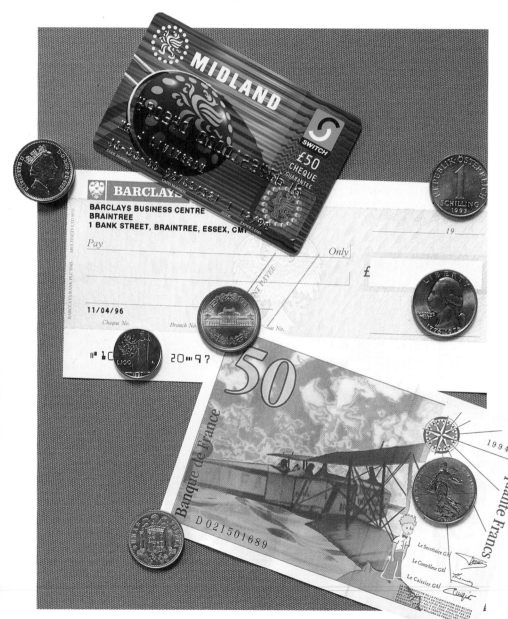

What is money?

Today, when we think of money we think of coins, banknotes, cheques and credit cards. Money has not always looked like this. People in the past have used many things, such as cows, salt and sea shells, as money. In fact, money can be **anything** that people are prepared to accept in payment.

Although anything acceptable can be money, some things are better than others. Ideally, money needs to be long-lasting and easy to carry around. It also needs to be worth the right amount to buy things with - oddly enough, it must not be too valuable. Diamonds would not be a sensible form of money - imagine trying to buy a bar of chocolate with one!

Eggs were used as money in 19th century Guatemala, but they would not normally be suitable because they break too easily and go bad quickly.

Large sheets of copper weighing up to 20 kg were made as money in the 17th century in Sweden. They soon went out of use, partly because they were so difficult to carry around.

The uses of money

Money is used for...
- buying and selling
- paying wages or pocket money
- paying taxes
- saving

The history of money

We do not know when money began. People probably had money long before they had writing to tell us about it. We only begin to have a good idea of how money developed once writing was invented about 4,500 years ago. This time-line picks out some of the highlights in the story of money.

2500 BC	by 2500 BC - clay tablets record silver being used to make payments in Mesopotamia, modern Iraq (pages 12-13)
2000	
1500	
1000	by 1000 BC - cowrie shell money in China (page 6)
500	by 600 BC - gold-silver alloy coins in ancient Turkey (page 6) bronze tool-shaped coins in China (page 6)
500	by AD 100 - Roman coins in use all over Europe (page 17)
1000	by AD 1000 - paper money in China (page 8)
1500	from AD 1535 - first coins made in the Americas (page 28) AD 1661 - first European banknotes in Sweden (page 9)
2000 AD	AD 1950 - first modern credit card in U.S.A. (page 35)

COINS

Coins have been the most important and common kind of money for more than 2,000 years. A coin is a small piece of metal made to be used as money. Today there are coins in almost every country in the world. They are normally round, but can be made in dozens of shapes and sizes.

Seven-sided coin of the United Kingdom.

Twelve-sided coin of the Solomon Islands.

Square coin of Malaya.

Triangular coin of the Cook Islands.

Round coin of the USA.

Making coins

People made early coins in two main ways. Most coins were made by **striking**. Small pieces of metal called blanks were heated up to soften them. The blanks were then stamped between two engraved tools (called 'dies') which pressed the design on to them. In Europe people made coins by hand in this way right up until the 17th century.

The first coins

Some of the very earliest coins were made more than 2,600 years ago in the 7th century BC, by the Greek and Lydian people who lived in what we now call western Turkey. These coins were simply small lumps of metal which were stamped with a design to show who had made them. They were made of an **alloy** (mixture) of gold and silver called electrum. People in Greece and other nearby countries soon copied them and started to make and use their own coins.

Electrum coin made in western Turkey from about 600 BC, stamped with a lion's head. (Enlarged.)

Find out more

Can you find western Turkey in an atlas?

Chinese coins

About the same time as coins began to be used in Turkey the Chinese invented a very different-looking coinage. Their coins were bronze and shaped like tools or small shells called cowries. The value of these coins was based on their weight. Some had the name of the place where they were made marked on them.

Knife-shaped coin

Cowrie shell

Some coins, like the Chinese ones, were made by **casting**. The coin-maker poured molten metal into coin-shaped moulds and then let it cool and harden. The advantage of making coins like this was that many coins could be cast at the same time.

One disadvantage was that coins made by casting were easier to forge (copy) than coins made by striking.

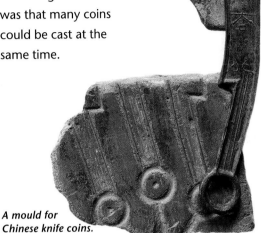

A mould for Chinese knife coins.

Three different forms of early Chinese coins in the shape of a hoe, a knife and a cowrie shell.

Cowrie-shaped coin

Profile: as rich as Croesus

Croesus (560-546 BC) was the last king of the Lydians of western Turkey. He was extremely successful in conquering the lands of his neighbours. This, together with precious metals from the rivers of Lydia, made him fabulously wealthy. He is still remembered in the expression 'as rich as Croesus'. We think Croesus was the first king to make coins of pure gold or silver, rather than electrum.

Gold coin of Croesus

PAPER MONEY

It can be very inconvenient to use coins, because one coin is not usually worth very much. Imagine how many coins would be needed to buy something expensive like a computer! This was often the reason that people in the past started using paper money. Another reason was that sometimes there was not enough metal to make all the coins that were needed. Like most coins, paper money has its value and the name of the authority that made it clearly marked on it.

This South African note is worth 20 Rand and is issued by the South African Reserve Bank.

(see page 5)

Europe

The first banknotes were not issued in Europe until about 300 years ago. In the middle of the 17th century Swedish money took the form of huge, heavy sheets of copper (see page 5). These were almost impossible to use for daily business. A solution was provided by a man called Johan Palmstruch. He suggested using pieces of paper to represent coins.

In Britain the Bank of England and the Bank of Scotland began to issue notes in the 1690s. British people still use notes from these two banks today!

The first notes

The very first paper money was made about 1,000 years ago in China. At the time, iron coins were the official money. Each coin was worth very little, and so a lot of heavy coins were needed to buy anything. Instead of carrying all their coins around, people left them with merchants, who issued receipts for the coins. These receipts were then used as money. They were the earliest form of paper currency.

Later, the Chinese government took over printing and issuing paper money.

Chinese paper money of the 14th century. In real life it is bigger than this page.

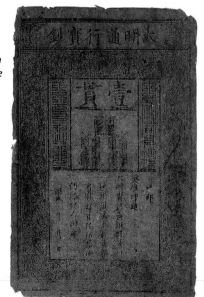

8

An early banknote from Sweden.

Can you see the Bank of England's promise on this old £5 note?

Profile: Johan Palmstruch

Although Johan Palmstruch invented the banknote in Europe, he did not receive many thanks for his new idea. He made the mistake of issuing lots of notes, but did not have enough gold and silver.

Customers, finding that they were unable to exchange their notes for coins, thought that the notes were not worth anything. As a result, his bank soon went out of business. For this he was sentenced to death! Fortunately, he was saved from execution by the king of Sweden.

Banknote printing works.

Promise to pay...

Paper money was originally issued by banks or individuals who promised to pay the owner of the note its full value in gold or silver coins if they wanted it. This helped people to believe the notes were valuable. English banknotes today still carry this promise, even though they can no longer be changed for gold and silver.

Making paper money

The first stage in making a banknote is to design it carefully. The designs are produced with a combination of careful hand-engraving, highly sophisticated machinery and computers. Then, a special hard-wearing paper is made from cotton fibres. Finally, the note is printed with special inks made from secret ingredients. Many notes carry portraits of famous people, or animals, or plants.

Different precautions are taken to make the note as hard to copy as possible (see page 35).

SALT, STONES AND PLASTIC

In the 14th century an Arab traveller called Ibn Battuta reported unusual money being used at an oasis in the Sahara desert in Africa. He wrote that the people there 'use salt in trade, as gold and silver are used elsewhere. They cut it up into bits and buy and sell with it.' Money has taken many forms at different times and in different places around the world, ranging from blocks of salt to stones and from shells to iron tools.

In some parts of Africa people used bars of salt as money right up until the 1920s.

Tribal money

In the 19th century European travellers were often puzzled when they saw people in distant lands making payments with things that were not coins. Two examples from the Pacific Islands were the stone money of Yap and the feather money of Santa Cruz. These were not used to buy and sell things, but were paid out when people got married or on other special occasions.

The 'money' of Santa Cruz. Small red feathers were glued on to long fibre strips up to 10 metres long.

Stones like this one from Yap could be as large as 3 metres across.

Everyday items

Many everyday items have been chosen for use as money in the past. People chose the things they thought were valuable: cocoa beans (Mexico), banana seeds (Uganda), lengths of telephone wire (Tanzania), blocks of wood (Angola), eggs (Guatemala) and lipstick (Vietnam).

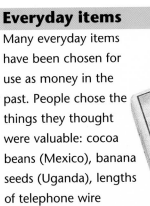

In the 1970s in Italy there were not enough small coins, and shop-keepers gave out sweets as change!

Everyday items have also been used as money in the 20th century in European countries. After the Second World War payments were often made with imported cigarettes in Germany.

Today

Today, people can pay for things or move money from one place to another without actually using real coins or notes. Money can be stored in the memory banks of computers, and easily swapped from one person's account to another. Often this is done with a bank card which allows people to check up on and use the money in their computer accounts. In some countries people now have bank cards with built-in computers. These are called **smart cards**.

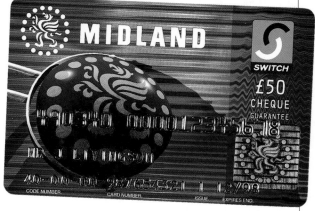

The latest development in the story of money is the introduction of **e-money**. E-money is a type of money stored and spent on the Internet, a system by which people can communicate with each other by computer. Using e-money it is possible to browse through the catalogues of shops thousands of miles away, choose an item, pay for it and wait for delivery without ever having left your home.

THE EARLIEST MONEY

We know roughly when the first coins and banknotes were made. Before that, people may have used other things as money. We have no idea what they used or when they started. Early money did not always look like the money we use today, so it is sometimes hard to recognise. We can guess that an object might have been used as money, but we do not know for certain. It is only when people started writing about money that we can be sure they were using it.

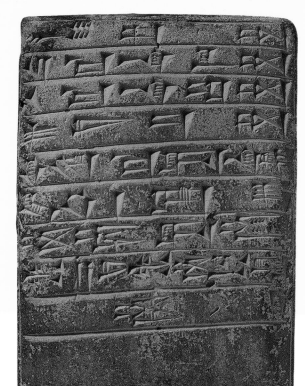

A Mesopotamian clay tablet from about 2,500 BC with cuneiform writing listing the prices of various goods in silver.

This duck-shaped weight from Mesopotamia was used to weigh silver. It is more than 4,000 years old.

Ancient Mesopotamia

The very first written evidence of money comes from Mesopotamia (present-day Iraq) and is about 4,500 years old. It is written in a script called cuneiform and tells how payments were made with weighed amounts of silver and baskets of barley. At first weighed silver and barley were not used to buy and sell, only to pay rent and taxes.

Ancient Egypt

The Egyptians also made payments with weighed metals. Evidence of this comes from writing on a stone monument at Giza, the site of the great pyramids.

These oddly-shaped pieces of silver from Egypt would have been used to make payments. Why do you think their shape does not matter?

This Egyptian wall painting from the 14th century *BC* shows gold rings being weighed on a balance. The weight is in the shape of a bull's head.

Aes rude

Before the Romans had coins (pages 16-17) they used lumps of bronze called **aes rude** ('unworked bronze') as money.

Aes rude from the 4th century BC.

Prehistoric money

Why would anybody make an axe that was not sharp or a tool out of crumbly chalk? Sometimes archaeologists find objects like these. Since almost anything acceptable can be used as money, it may be that such items were types of money. Perhaps they were paid out at weddings or on other important occasions. Prehistoric jewellery may have been used as money too. These torcs, or neck-rings, were found at Ipswich in eastern England.

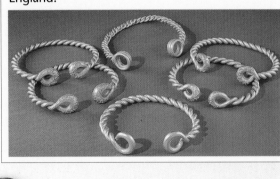

THE ANCIENT GREEKS

The ancient Greeks played a vital role in the early history of coins. As well as making some of the world's earliest coins (page 6), they were the first people to use coins extensively in trade. Many Greek coins were very skilfully made, and extremely beautiful. They have had an important influence on coin design right up to the present day.

Greek silver coin from Agrigentum.

City states

Ancient Greece was made up of a number of separate city states. Each city state was independent of the others and had its own badge, which could be used to mark its coins. The city of Aegina was on an island and so it chose a sea creature, a turtle, for its badge.

Gods and goddesses

The ancient Greeks believed in many gods and goddesses. Some Greek cities put the portrait of their patron god or goddess on their coins.

This is a portrait of Zeus, the most important god of the Greeks. It is on a silver coin from the city of Elis.

Copies

Once the Greeks had started to use coins, the idea quickly spread to the rest of the Mediterranean world. Many Greek coins were copied by people who were not Greeks. Can you see any differences between this Greek coin from Athens and the coins copied from it?

Egyptian copy

Arabian copy

Italian copy

Turkish copy

Profile: Alexander the Great

Alexander the Great appears on many Greek coins. He was one of the most successful generals who has ever lived. He became the ruler of the small Greek kingdom of Macedonia at the age of 20. By the time he died at only 33 he had conquered a huge empire that stretched from Greece to India. Many of the kings who came after Alexander the Great put his picture on their coins. They believed he was a god.

A silver coin showing Alexander as a god.

THE ROMANS

The Romans began making coins in about 300 BC (over 2,000 years ago). They got the idea from the Greeks. Roman silver and gold coins were similar to Greek ones, but the Romans also used large bars of bronze as money.

Rome had begun as a small village on the banks of the River Tiber in Italy but in time it became the centre of one of the greatest empires the world has ever seen. The same system of coins was used over nearly all of this huge empire.

According to a legend, twins called Romulus and Remus founded (began) the city of Rome in 753 BC. Romulus and Remus were brought up in the wild by a wolf.

A bronze sculpture of the wolf with Romulus and Remus.

Many Roman coins show the legend of Romulus and Remus.

Part of a Roman bronze bar from about 300 BC.

3rd century BC

Coins can be influential

The Romans used the pictures on their coins to express ideas. The Roman ruler Julius Caesar was murdered in 44 BC. One of his killers, a man called Brutus, produced this coin. He hoped to convince the Roman people that it was a good thing to kill Caesar. The coin shows two daggers and a **pileus** (a kind of hat). In Rome these hats were given to freed slaves as a symbol of freedom.

2nd century AD

16

Travelling coins!

Roman coins are found wherever the Romans went. Some Roman coins were used far beyond the frontiers of the Roman Empire in places like India and Russia. The map shows some of the places where archaeologists have found Roman coins. (The Roman Empire is coloured red.)

Find out more Look at this map and use an atlas to find out the modern names of some of the places where Roman coins have been found.

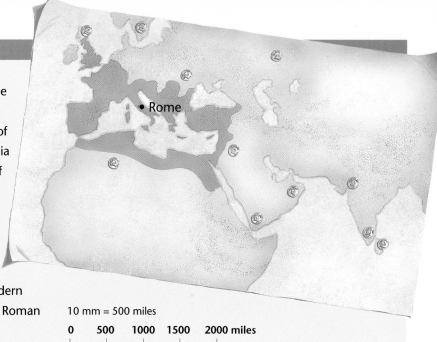

Rome

10 mm = 500 miles

0   500   1000   1500   2000 miles

Roman money

From the first century AD, the Romans had a full set of coins of different values, made of different metals, just like ours. The most valuable coin was made of gold and was called an **aureus**. Their main silver coin was called a **denarius**. An aureus was worth 25 denarii and was too valuable for most people to use every day. There were also five different types of bronze or brass coins, known as a **sestertius**, a **dupondius**, an **as**, a **semis** and a **quadrans**. A single gold aureus was worth 1600 quadrantes of copper!

Aureus

Denarius

Sestertius

As

Semis

Dupondius

Quadrans

The Roman army

One of the main reasons the Romans made coins was to pay their soldiers. The Romans needed a strong army to control the empire. A Roman soldier at the time of the Emperor Augustus (27 BC - AD 14) earned 225 silver denarii a year.

This denarius commemorates the 17th legion of the Roman army.

THE MIDDLE AGES

The Middle Ages is the name historians give to the time from the 5th to the 16th centuries. Coins changed a lot during this period. The Middle Ages began with the fall of the Roman Empire. Now western Europe was no longer controlled by one strong state. Through the thousand years of the Middle Ages, many new states grew up and most of them had their own coins. Even individual cities and bishops sometimes made their own coins.

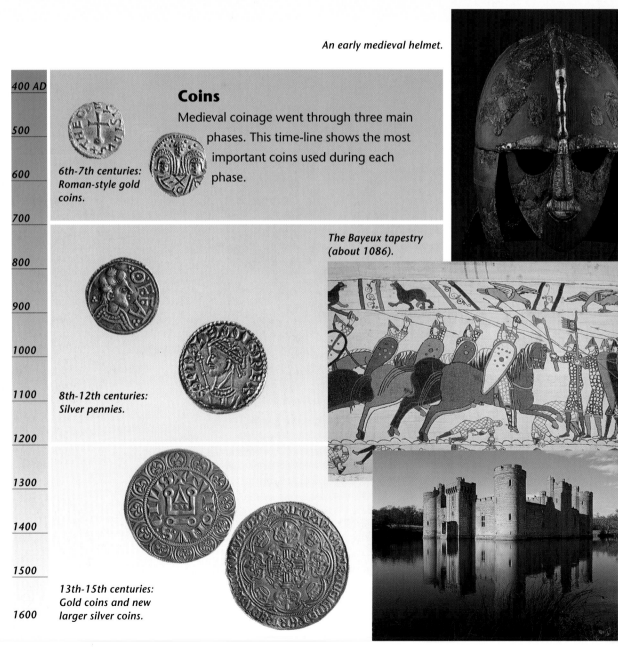

An early medieval helmet.

Coins

Medieval coinage went through three main phases. This time-line shows the most important coins used during each phase.

6th-7th centuries: Roman-style gold coins.

The Bayeux tapestry (about 1086).

8th-12th centuries: Silver pennies.

13th-15th centuries: Gold coins and new larger silver coins.

400 AD	
500	
600	
700	
800	
900	
1000	
1100	
1200	
1300	
1400	
1500	
1600	

A 13th century castle.

A money changer from a medieval manuscript

Money changers

These different types of coins were used in the same area in the 15th century. Money changers exchanged one type of money for another, a bit like a bank does today. And just like a bank they made you pay to have your money changed.

The church

In the Middle Ages Christianity was the religion of the whole of western Europe. Many beautiful churches and cathedrals were built. Some bishops, archbishops and abbeys produced their own coins, like this one.

The Vikings

The Vikings were a race of travelling people who lived in Scandinavia in the Middle Ages. They are famous for their longships and they sailed all over the known world. Sometimes they attacked towns and monasteries to steal treasure from them. But very often they also sailed on trading voyages, exchanging items like furs and walrus tusks for silver coins. The Vikings eventually settled in many parts of Europe in countries as far apart as England, Italy and Russia.

This is a hoard of Viking silver found at Cuerdale in Lancashire, England.

THE RENAISSANCE

Coins changed a great deal in the two or three centuries after the Middle Ages. These changes were linked to other changes in ways of thought, in what people wrote, and in painting and architecture. In particular, people started to look back and admire the classical civilizations of ancient Greece and Rome. So many changes happened at this time that the period was called the Renaissance, a French word that means 'rebirth'.

The Artistic Renaissance

There was a growing interest in Greek and Roman art during the Renaissance. You can see this on the coins of the period which were the first since the Roman Empire to use life-like portraits.

Silver groat of Edward III, 1351-1360.

The king on this Medieval coin does not look very realistic...

Silver testoon of Henry VII, 1504-1509.

...unlike the ruler on this coin of the Renaissance.

Machinery

The first machine-made coins were produced during the 16th century. Early coin making machines were powered by water, animals or even by people.

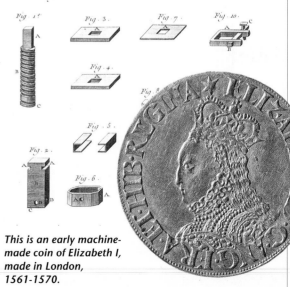

This is an early machine-made coin of Elizabeth I, made in London, 1561-1570.

Silver

The discovery of some very large silver mines, in Mexico and Peru as well as in Europe, changed the whole European money system. It was now based on silver coins called **testoons** and exceptionally large silver coins often called **thalers**. The word thaler was pronounced 'dollar' in English. Copper money also came into use again for the first time since the Romans.

thaler

testoon

copper cavallo

A picture of a silver mine on a 4 thaler German coin.

Banks

A bank is a place where people leave their money to keep it safe. As well as taking care of money, banks **invest** it (they use it to earn more money). Banks have existed for thousands of years, but the first really large banks appeared during the Renaissance. In the 16th century a German banking family named Fugger acquired a massive fortune through its banking activities.

Jakob Fugger and his secretary. In the background you can see a list of all Fugger's banking houses.

ASIA

Asia is the world's largest continent. It includes huge countries like China and India. China was one of the first countries in the world to make coins. They invented coins quite separately from the Greeks in Turkey, but at about the same time (in the 7th century BC). China's early coins were shaped like cowrie shells and tools (see pages 6-7). From China coins spread to Japan, Korea and Vietnam. People in India got the idea of coins from the Greeks, and began to make their own coins in the 4th century BC.

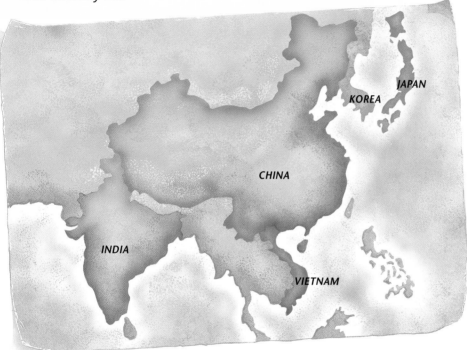

In the mid-17th century the Chinese authorities were making up to 2,000 million cash coins every year!

If this number of coins were strung together they would reach more than 300 times higher than the world's tallest mountain, Mount Everest.

If they were laid out side by side, they would run for 22 times the 1,400 mile length of the Great Wall of China.

And if they were piled up they would weigh as much as 1,600 Asian elephants.

Cash

China's early coins were gradually replaced by round coins with holes in the middle. We call these round coins **cash**. The earliest cash were issued by the first Chinese emperor in 221 BC. Similar coins were still in use at the beginning of the 20th century, more than 2,000 years later.

Why do you think Chinese cash had holes in them?
It was so that they could be threaded on to a string and carried easily.

118 BC

AD 1909

Japan

Japan got the idea of making coins from China. The first Japanese coins, from AD 708, looked just like Chinese ones.

An early Japanese coin.

In later centuries Japan issued coins which were not copied from the Chinese. This rectangular silver **bu** and oval gold **oban** were both made in the middle of the 19th century. The gold oban has its denomination and mint mark added in ink.

Silver bu.

Gold oban, shown smaller than life size.

India

The first Indian coins, made in the 4th century BC, were weighed pieces of silver stamped with punch-marks. A little later, cast square coins were used. This one has an Indian elephant on one side.

From the 13th century AD many Indian coins were influenced by the religion of Islam (pages 24-25).

Modern Indian coins look very much like European ones.

50 paise coin (India, 1985).

ISLAM

Islam is the religion revealed to the Prophet Muhammad at Mecca in Arabia in the early 7th century AD. The first Islamic coins were copied from the coins of people in present-day Iran, Iraq, Egypt and Syria, who were conquered by Arabs.

Early Islamic coin   *The Iranian coin it was based upon.*

Inscriptions

Some Muslim people thought it was wrong to show pictures of people and animals. After AD 696 most Islamic coins only had writing on them.

The writing on some Islamic coins became very elaborate and beautiful. Writing instead of pictures was used as decoration. The Arabic script on this coin is called **Kufic**.

This later coin is decorated with a different kind of Arabic writing called cursive script.

An example of Kufic script carved on a tombstone from Egypt. It reads 'In the name of God the merciful'.

The 20th century

In the 20th century a number of Arab countries have put pictures on their coins.

Modern Islamic coins from Libya and Iraq.

Coin of Libya with portrait of a king.   *Coin of Iraq, showing palm trees.*

Dates

In Christian countries people count dates from the birth of Jesus Christ. Islamic dates are reckoned from the flight (Hijra) of the prophet Muhammad from Mecca to the city of Medina. This means that the Islamic year 1 is AD 622 on the Christian calendar.

Find out more

These are the numbers 1 to 10 in Arabic.

Can you read the Islamic date on this coin?

Answer: AH 1277

Profile: Saladin

A statue of Saladin in Damascus.

Saladin, Sultan of Egypt and Syria, was a great leader of the Arabs in the 12th century. For years he fought against invading armies of Christians known as 'crusaders'. Saladin is still remembered by Arabs for his wisdom and for the fine citadels, roads and hospitals he built.

A gold coin of Saladin.

AFRICA

The first coins in Africa were Greek coins made in the late 6th century BC. Other types of money (such as weighed metal in Egypt) were common long before that. The first parts of Africa to start using coins were the areas near the Mediterranean Sea, which were mostly ruled by the Greeks and Romans. Some areas of Africa did not start making their own coins until as late as the 1950s. In the 19th and 20th centuries many African countries were under European control. This caused European-type coins and banknotes to spread throughout Africa.

Manilla bronze ring.

Early days

These are some of the coins used in Africa. The first African coins were made in Libya 2,500 years ago. Some of the most impressive African coins were made about two centuries later by a family called the Ptolemies, who ruled Egypt for about 300 years. The last of the Ptolemies was called Cleopatra.

The Romans defeated Cleopatra in war in 31 BC. Then the Romans started to produce their own coins in North Africa. Later on, the Byzantine Empire and then the Muslims (see pages 24-25) controlled parts of Africa, and made their own coins there.

Find out more Cleopatra had a fascinating life. See if you can find out about it from an encyclopedia or another book.

An early Greek coin made in Libya in the 6th century BC.

This Roman gold aureus shows wild beasts being rounded up for the circus in Rome.

A silver tetradrachm of Cleopatra.

An Islamic coin from North Africa, 11th century AD.

A 1000 franc note from French Equatorial Africa.

African money

Many things have been used as money in different parts of Africa.

In Western Africa bronze rings called **manillas** were used to make payments from the 13th century right up until 1948. People from Europe made their own manillas for trading with the Africans. This one was made in Birmingham, England.

Cattle have been used to make payments in East Africa. We know that the Greeks, Romans and Celts also used cattle in this way.

Modern money

This coin from Uganda was issued after Uganda gained independence from Britain. It still uses the old British denomination of shillings.

Can you guess which country controlled the Malagasy Republic, which issued this 10 franc piece in 1991?

Answer: France

Zambia did not start to have its own coins until 1953. It was then a British colony called Northern Rhodesia. This penny dates from 1961.

THE AMERICAS

The Vikings in America

The very first coins in the Americas were brought by Vikings who had sailed from Greenland. Only one example has ever been found. It was discovered on an Indian site in Maine and dates from the 11th century AD.

A Viking coin like the one found in America.

The Incas

Many modern South American coins and notes have pictures of ancient peoples like the Incas. The Incas were a South American people who set up a remarkably well-organized empire that covered large areas of the continent. They had no coins, but they valued shells more than gold. In the 16th century the Incas were conquered by Europeans in search of gold and silver.

A Spanish coin made from Peruvian silver in 1769.

Wampum

When the first Europeans arrived in North America they found the Native Americans using shell beads called wampum to make payments. These beads were made into decorative belts (**below**)

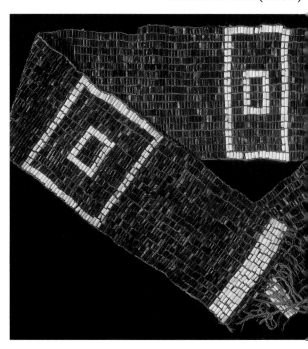

An Inca man on a modern banknote from Peru.

and exchanged on important occasions. For a while wampum was adopted by the European settlers as their own currency. They also used tobacco leaves and animal skins as money.

Today

America's dollar is the most widely-used currency in the world. All recent American coins have the portrait of a president as their main design. Most American coins also have the inscriptions IN GOD WE TRUST, LIBERTY and E PLURIBUS UNUM on them. Liberty refers to freedom from the rule of Britain. America won this freedom after fighting the War of Independence in the late 18th century. E Pluribus Unum is Latin. It means 'one from many', which is what happened when all the states of North America joined together to become one country, the United States.

The gold rush

After people discovered large amounts of gold in California in the mid-19th century, they started to produce many gold coins. One of the largest was this $50 coin, which weighs almost 85 g.

Statue of Lincoln in the Lincoln Memorial.

Profile: Abraham Lincoln

Abraham Lincoln, sixteenth president of America, was the first person ever to appear on a regular coin of the United States. He has always been highly respected for making sure that all the states of America stayed together as one country, even though this involved fighting a civil war. He is also famous for the stand he took against slavery. The front of the cent shows Abraham Lincoln's stern portrait and the back shows his Memorial in Washington.

MONEY TALKS

Historians can learn fascinating things about the past by looking very carefully at coins. People have been studying old coins since the Renaissance (see pages 20-21). Sometimes looking at coins can even tell historians things that they cannot find out in any other way.

Musical instruments

Look closely at this Indian coin from the 4th century AD. The man on it is playing an unusual form of stringed instrument, similar to a harp. None of these instruments exist today.

Mint marks

A mint is a factory where coins are made. Looking closely at coins can sometimes tell us which mint made them. This penny of George V of England (1910-36) has a tiny mint mark which tells us it was made at Kings Norton, Birmingham. Can you see it?

Find out more Look at some modern coins. How many of them have mint marks?

Faces from the past

Coins also tell historians a lot about what people in the past looked like. This is a portrait of a Gaulish chieftain on a Roman coin.

This gold coin of Elizabeth I of England shows her beautiful crown and neck ruff ....

....while these ancient Greek coins show that hairstyles in the 5th century BC were as varied as they are today!

Careful study of coins can be very rewarding

Some rulers are only known from the coins they issued. Silbannacus was a rebel Roman emperor. We only know about him because of two coins which have his name on them.

Rare silver coin of Silbannacus.

Can you read his name on this coin?

Roman buildings

Many Roman coins have pictures of buildings on them. Some of these are very detailed. Because of this they can give us a good idea of what the buildings looked like, even if they disappeared many years ago.

An artist's drawing of what the Arch of Nero in Rome would have looked like. The arch itself was pulled down long ago. This precise drawing was made by studying pictures of Nero's arch on Roman coins.

Bullion marks

This large gold coin of the English Queen Anne (1702-14) was made from gold captured from Spanish ships at a place called Vigo Bay. This is recorded below the queen's picture on the left.

Find out more choose a current coin and see if you can find out where it was made.

A captured Spanish ship.

COINS AND THE ARCHAEOLOGIST

Archaeologists gain valuable information about the past from studying where ancient coins are found. If they know exactly where a coin was found they may be able to say who owned the coin, when it was made and what it was used for.

These archaeologists are uncovering a large hoard of Roman gold and silver coins at Hoxne in Suffolk, eastern England.

Dating

When archaeologists excavate a site they identify layers of earth called **strata**. Each layer represents a different period of time. The oldest layers are at the bottom and the most recent ones are at the top. If archaeologists find a coin within a layer it helps them to date the other finds in the same layer.

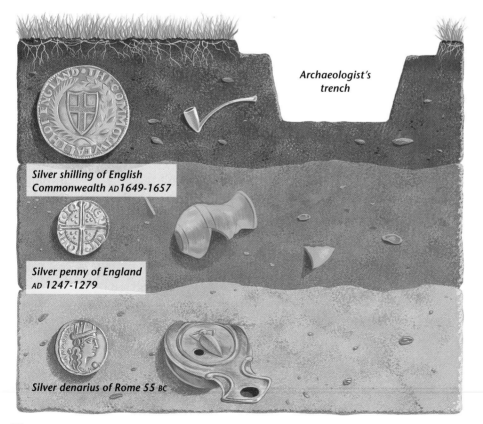

Archaeologist's trench

Silver shilling of English Commonwealth AD 1649-1657

Silver penny of England AD 1247-1279

Silver denarius of Rome 55 BC

Important rulers

Marking the places where ancient coins are found can give archaeologists some idea of the importance of the ruler who issued the coins.

Cunobelin was a king in southern Britain in the years before the Roman invasion of AD 43. This map shows that his coins have been found over a large area shown in dark green. This suggests that he was important and influential.

Trade

Coins found by archaeologists sometimes provide evidence of ancient trade. In the Middle Ages, many Italian merchants travelled to trade fairs in the Champagne region of France. As a result, archaeologists in France often find Italian coins.

Thousands of Roman coins have been found in southern India. Roman merchants traded them for Indian jewels, spices and other luxuries (see pages 16-17).

Roman coins and spices.

Gold coin of Cunobelin.

Feature: Archaeology, the future

In the future archaeologists may be able to find out even more from the coins they excavate. This is a computer-generated diagram of an archaeological site at Shepton Mallet (Somerset, England). The excavators of the site have used advanced electronic equipment to record precisely where they found each coin and other items. By looking carefully at this information they may be able to work out exactly who was using the coins. For example, if they found coins with women's weaving equipment more often than with other objects, it might show that women used coins more than men did.

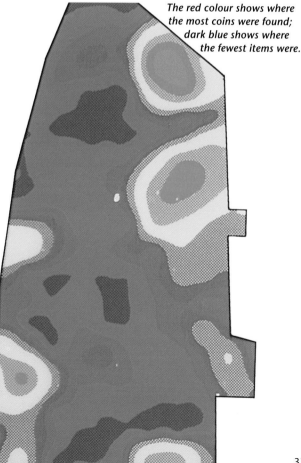

The red colour shows where the most coins were found; dark blue shows where the fewest items were.

PAST AND PRESENT

Coins and banknotes have developed over a long period. Many aspects of modern coins and banknotes have their origins far back in history. Have you ever stopped to think where the picture on a coin came from, or how the pound got its name?

Names

Many coins have been named after a weight. The Italian lira is a good example. Its name goes back to the ancient Roman **libra** (a pound in weight) which was the basis of all Roman money. The British pound is so-called because it originally meant a pound of silver. The pound sign (£) also comes from the Roman word libra; it is just a crossed letter 'L'.

This early Roman coin weighed a pound.

National symbols

The national symbol of the United States is the bald eagle. It appeared on some of the earliest US coins made in 1794, and is still used on modern quarter dollar coins.

A modern 'quarter' of the US.

On the back of this British 50 pence piece you will see a seated figure wearing a helmet and carrying a trident and an olive branch. Her name is Britannia, and she is a symbol for Great Britain. Britannia is not a new figure on coins. She first appeared on coins of the Roman emperors.

A British 50 pence coin.

Britannia on a Roman bronze coin.

The humble penny

The smallest current British coin, the penny, is also the longest-lasting. It has been part of British money since the 8th century AD - 1200 years ago.

A penny of Alfred the Great (AD 871-901).

The first pennies were about the same size as a modern penny but were made of silver. By the 18th century pennies were being made of less valuable metals. This copper penny of George III (1760-1820) weighed 28 g, nearly ten times more than the penny today.

King George III penny.

Legends

The inscription on a coin is called a legend. The first coins with legends were made in western Turkey in about 600 BC. They were inscribed in Greek with the words 'I am the badge of Phanes'. Today, every coin has a legend.

This 19th century note of credit promised to pay a sum of more than £283 in three months' time.

Banknotes

Some of the security features protecting modern banknotes from forgery have been in use for hundreds of years. Watermarked paper was introduced in 1666, almost as soon as banknotes began to be used in Europe. American notes do not have watermarks, but since the 1840s they have been made with paper containing coloured fibres. It is very hard for forgers to copy paper with watermarks or coloured fibres (see pages 8-9 and 36-37).

Credit notes and credit cards

The earliest equivalent to credit cards were 'notes of credit', which have been used by merchants for many hundreds of years. A note of credit is a written promise to pay for goods in the future.

An American banknote made with paper containing coloured fibres. On the right-hand side is a warning to anyone who tries to forge the note.

Modern credit cards began in America in the 1920s. Oil companies, hotels and other firms started issuing them to trustworthy customers. The customers could buy petrol or pay for a hotel room without using cash or a cheque.

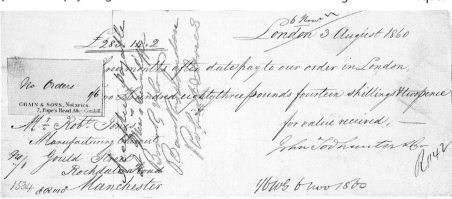

FORGERY

We all know that coins represent an accepted form and amount of money. Every shop-keeper knows how much each coin is worth and is happy to accept it. As a result, people began to forge coins as soon as they became widely used. Forgers made fake coins of a cheap metal plated with gold or silver so it looked like a solid gold or silver coin. In more recent times people have tried to make clever copies of banknotes. One of the biggest forgeries of all time was carried out by the German Secret Service in the Second World War. They forged £150 million in British £5 notes!

A plated Roman coin. If you look carefully, you can see that only a thin layer of silver covers a cheap metal core.

Testing

The only way to be absolutely certain that a coin or note is not a forgery is to test it. Modern notes can be tested with hand-held electronic machines. In the past coins were tested by cutting them, or by weighing.

This ancient coin from Athens has been cut to make sure it is solid silver.

A 17th century pair of scales made for testing the weight of British gold coins.

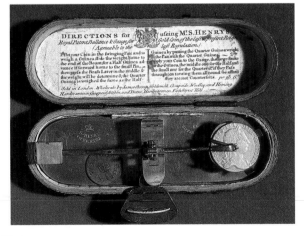

The pound coin

The Latin inscription around the edge of some British pound coins reads DECUS ET TUTAMEN, meaning 'a decoration and a protection'.

These words have appeared on the edge of a number of coins from the time of Charles II, king of Great Britain (1660-85). They were originally designed to be a protection against clipping and other damage to the metal.

Preventing forgery

From the 17th century many coins have had milled (marked) edges. This makes them harder to copy and stops anybody clipping off bits of metal.

The milled edge of a British 10 pence piece.

Clippings cut from English silver shillings of Edward VI (1547-53) and Charles I (1625-49).

Modern notes have very complicated and detailed patterns to make them difficult to forge. They may also have watermarks or holograms and tiny deliberate mistakes in their designs to try to catch forgers out.

Terrible punishments

The profit to be made from forgery has always been high. But so has the punishment if you are caught! Forgers in medieval Germany were boiled alive in oil, while those in Russia had molten lead poured down their throats. Moneyers found guilty of dishonesty in the 10th century English kingdom of Athelstan were punished by having a hand cut off and nailed above the door of the mint.

This pretend note was made by a cartoonist called Cruikshank in the early 19th century. He was protesting about the severity of the punishment for people using forged notes, and he hoped this pretend note would embarrass the government. Look at the signature. Jack Ketch was the official hangman.

The detail on this 35 kyats note from Burma makes it difficult to copy.

HOARDING

How do you keep your money safe? Probably by keeping it in a bank or savings account. But how would you keep money safe if there were no banks? This was the problem faced by people all over the world until the 19th and 20th centuries when banks became common. The solution most people came up with was to hide their money away, usually by burying it in the ground.

This is a 15th century picture of a man burying a hoard of coins.

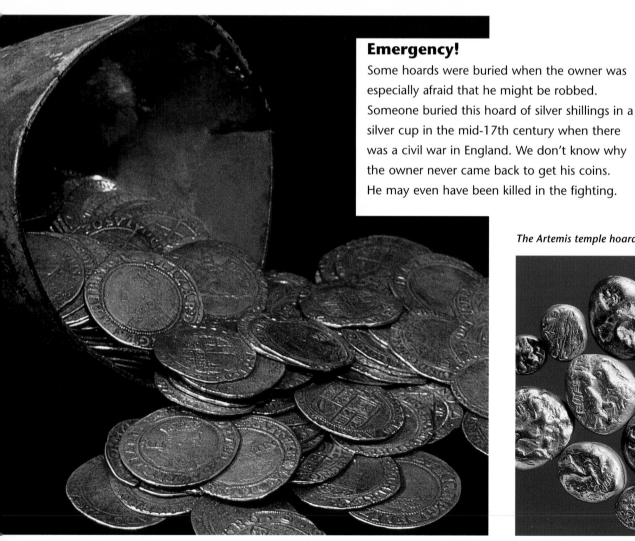

Emergency!

Some hoards were buried when the owner was especially afraid that he might be robbed. Someone buried this hoard of silver shillings in a silver cup in the mid-17th century when there was a civil war in England. We don't know why the owner never came back to get his coins. He may even have been killed in the fighting.

The Artemis temple hoard.

Money for the gods

Occasionally, hoards are found which appear to have been buried as offerings to gods or goddesses. The oldest hoard ever found, from Ephesus in Turkey, seems to have been a gift to the Greek goddess Artemis. It was buried under the foundations of her temple more than 2500 years ago.

A statue of Artemis from Ephesus.

Sunken treasure

Under the sea, archaeologists have sometimes found the remains of ships that sank with large quantities of coins or precious metals on board. This fabulous treasure, including more than 1,500 large gold coins and 40 gold ingots and bars, was found in 1992. Divers discovered the treasure in a shipwreck off the coast of Uruguay in South America.

Buried treasure!

Spanish treasure ships carrying silver coins called **pieces of eight** and gold coins called **doubloons** from America to Europe were sometimes captured by pirates. The pirates hid their plunder, often by burying it on one of the small islands of the West Indies.

Pieces of eight and doubloons.

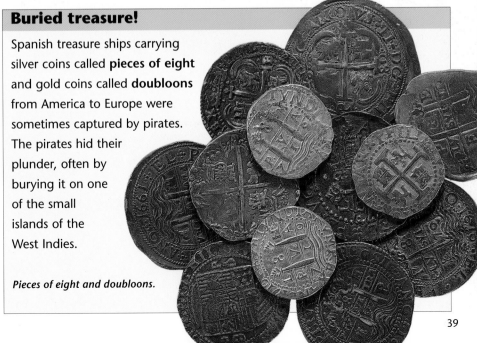

THE MAGIC OF MONEY

Coins and banknotes have often been seen as symbols of good luck. This is partly because most people think that having no money is unlucky! However, there is another more magical and mysterious side to money. There are many superstitions and beliefs about its power to do good. Since ancient times coins have been used to keep away evil, to protect men from death in battle and even to ensure true love.

This Chinese long life charm includes a rat, one of the Chinese birth signs.

Magic charms

Certain coins are regarded as lucky charms because of the pictures or writing on them. A lucky Indian coin is the Akbar rupee. It is a copy of the coins of the Moghul emperor Akbar (1556-1605) and has a statement of Islamic beliefs written on it.

In China, the making of coin-shaped charms can be traced right back to the 2nd century BC. Many designs are known, mostly with inscriptions wishing their user long life and wealth, or protection from evil spirits.

Disease and injury

Coins have been used to protect their owners' health. In medieval Germany special silver coins with a cross on one side were thought to protect people from the plague.

In medieval England people believed that a king could heal certain diseases. A person healed by the king would be given a special coin. This ceremony was called 'touching'.

A gold coin called an angel, used in the 'touching' ceremony.

A German coin showing St George and the dragon.

During the wars with France in the 17th century, a German officer miraculously escaped death when a bullet struck his lucky St. George coin. This led to a rush to carry similar 'lucky' coins by soldiers for many years afterwards.

The gods

Gifts to the gods have often been placed in water. In the Roman period water shrines were enormously popular. Archaeologists found one at Hadrian's Wall in northern England which contained thousands of bronze coins. This tradition is still carried on today. People throw coins into 'wishing wells', hoping that their dreams will come true.

Charon the ferryman

Many cultures have believed that dead people must be buried with enough money to pay for the journey to the afterlife. In ancient Greece, it was normal to place a coin in the mouth of a corpse. This was to pay Charon the ferryman who transported the dead across the river Styx to Hades (the kingdom of the dead). A ghost without the correct fare was doomed to wander forever on the wrong side of the river. Similar coins have been found with bodies in central Asia, in Afghanistan, and even in 17th century Romania, showing how widespread this belief was.

An Anglo-Saxon king buried at Sutton Hoo was also buried with enough money to transport him into the afterlife. Instead of one coin, though, he had 40 coins and two metal ingots. The coins were to pay the 40 oarsmen of the large boat he was buried in. The metal ingots were special payments for the boat's two steersmen to make sure he did not get lost!

Sutton Hoo gold coins and ingot.

GIFTS

Not all money is made for buying and selling. Some coins are produced especially to be given away.

The largest coins ever made were issued by the Moghul emperor Jahangir in India in the 17th century. You can see an example on pages 44-45. An Indian historian wrote that these coins were so big and valuable that they were kept under the palace in 'deep caves, supported by vast marble pillars'. They were much too large to use in trade. Jahangir probably gave them to important visitors as extravagant presents. He also made much smaller gold coins which were gifts. This one (shown enlarged) has Jahangir's portrait on one side.

A gold coin of Jahangir.

Roman generosity

Roman emperors used occasions like their birthdays to show their generosity. They gave away large sums of money, and put on shows for the Roman citizens to enjoy. This Roman gold solidus shows the emperor Valentinian I scattering coins from his chariot.

Find out more
Most books about the Romans will have more information about the wonderful shows put on by Roman emperors.

Maundy money

On Maundy Thursday in 1213 King John of England gave thirteen pence each to thirteen poor men. Since then it has been a tradition for kings and queens of England to give away Maundy money once a year.

These Maundy coins were given away by Queen Elizabeth II.

Queen Victoria

This gold £5 piece shows Queen Victoria guiding a lion, which represents Britain. The coin was never used by the public, but the Queen liked to give examples of it to her favourite guests.

Love tokens

Couples in the late medieval period exchanged coins as a symbol of their true love. In the 18th century this tradition gave way to a new one of exchanging specially engraved or decorated tokens. One or both sides of a coin was rubbed smooth, and it was carefully engraved with the initials of the lovers or with a symbol like a heart.

Convicts who were transported from Britain to far-away prison colonies like Australia often gave these tokens to the loved ones they had to leave behind.

Later on, these tokens became especially popular in America, where they are sometimes still made.

This love token is engraved 'Love till death'...

...and this convict token reads, 'When this you see, pray think on me'.

Wedding gifts

People have always given money or presents to couples getting married. in the 19th and 20th centuries in China it was normal to give pieces of silver (called **ingots**) or dollar coins.

A silver dollar used as wedding gift in China.

In parts of the Arab world a 'money hat' was an important part of a wedding. The hat was a headdress with dozens – or even hundreds – of coins sewn into it. The coins were a payment from the bridegroom's father to the bride's father.

Today, in some countries, people still give cash gifts to the bride and groom.

A 'money hat'.

The biggest and smallest

One of the biggest coins ever produced was this huge 1000 mohur gold coin from India. It is 5,967,900 times heavier than the coin beside it, which is a quarter jawa from Nepal. The 1000 mohur is also the world's most valuable coin. It is estimated to be worth about $10,000,000!

The largest denomination banknote was a 100,000,000,000,000 (one hundred thousand billion) pengo note issued in Hungary in 1946. One of the smallest was this 1 cent note from Hong Kong.

Silver jawas and a quarter jawa (actual size).

A one hundred thousand billion pengo note.

The cost

The most expensive land in the world is around the Meijiya Building in central Tokyo. In October 1988 it was valued by the Japanese National Land Agency at 33 million yen, or 248 thousand American dollars, per square metre.

In 1803 the state of Louisiana was sold by France to the United States of America. The total price was about $27 million, or just four cents an acre.

The rarest

There are a number of coins which are unique (only one exists).

This is a unique Roman gold coin from 28 BC.

There are also many coins of which we only have a few examples. This is an English penny from the year 1933. Only seven are known to exist. In 1994 one of the seven was sold at auction for more than £25,000.

The wealthiest

The richest person in the world is thought to have assets of about 37 billion dollars ($37,000,000,000).

Millionaires are not as rare as they used to be. It is estimated that one in every 250 people in the United States has at least $1,000,000. That is more than one million millionaires in one country!

Tokyo, Japan.

COLLECTING AND LEARNING

Collecting coins or banknotes can be a fascinating hobby, especially if you learn about the coins you collect. Why not begin by gathering together as many foreign coins as you can? Perhaps your parents have coins left over from when you have been on holiday abroad. Also, you might be surprised by how cheap some old coins are.

What to collect

Once you have been collecting for a while you will probably decide you want to specialize.

You might want to collect the coins of one country or period of history. Alternatively, you might want to collect coins or notes with particular pictures on them. You could collect a 'zoo' of coins with animals, or a 'city' of coins with buildings.

Find out more

The best thing about collecting coins is trying to learn about them. What denomination are they? What could you buy with them in the country they come from? What are the pictures on them?

If you ever collect any old coins, whether they are 50 or 500 years old, try to find out about the history of their time. This book is a good place to start, and there are names of other helpful books on page 48.

Why not visit your local museum? Many museums have collections of coins. The biggest collections are in the British Museum in London, which has a new money gallery, and in the Smithsonian in Washington.

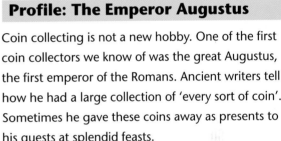

Gold coins in the British Museum.

Profile: The Emperor Augustus

Coin collecting is not a new hobby. One of the first coin collectors we know of was the great Augustus, the first emperor of the Romans. Ancient writers tell how he had a large collection of 'every sort of coin'. Sometimes he gave these coins away as presents to his guests at splendid feasts.

A cameo of the Emperor Augustus.

INDEX

aes rude 13
Africa 10, 26-27
Akbar rupee 40
Alexander the Great 15
alloy 6
angel 40
animal skins 29
archaeologists 13, 17, 32-33, 39, 41
as 17
Asia 22-23
Arabs 10, 24-25
Augustus 17, 47
aureus 17, 26

bank cards 11
banknotes 4, 5, 8-9, 35, 36, 37, 44, 46
banks 9, 19, 21, 38
biggest 44
Britain 8, 32, 34, 36, 43
Britannia 34
bronze 6, 13, 16, 27
bu 23
buildings on coins 31, 46

casting 7
cavallo 21
cent 29, 34, 44
Charon the ferryman 41
cheques 4
China 5, 6-7, 8, 22, 40, 43
Chinese cash 22
Christianity 19
Cleopatra 26
clippings 36
coin making 6-7, 20, 30
collecting 46-47
convicts 43
copies - see forgery
copper 5, 21, 34
cowrie shells 5, 6-7, 22
credit cards 35
credit notes 35
Croesus 7
Cruikshank 37
cuneiform 12
Cunobelin 32, 33

dating 25, 32
denarius 17
dollar 21, 29
doubloons 39

dupondius 17

E-money 11
Egypt 12, 13, 26
electrum 6,7
Elizabeth I 30
Ephesus 39

feather money 10
forgery 35, 36-37, 47
franc 27
Fugger, Jakob 21

gifts 39, 42-43, 47
gods and goddesses 14, 39, 41
gold 7, 9, 17, 18, 28, 29, 32, 36, 39, 42
gold rush 29
Greece 14-15, 20, 41
Greeks 14-15, 16, 26

Hijra 25
historians 30
hoarding 38-39

Ibn Battuta 10
Incas 28
India 22-23, 33, 42
ingots 39, 41
inscriptions 29
Islam 23, 24-25, 26

Jahangir 42
Japan 22-23, 45
Julius Caesar 16

Kings Norton 30
Korea 22

legends 35
libra 34
Lincoln, Abraham 29
lira 34
love tokens 43
Lydian coins 6

machine-made coins 20
magic charms 40
manillas 26-27
Maundy money 43
Mediterranean 15, 16-17, 18-19, 20-21, 22-23, 24-

25, 26
Mesopotamia 12
Middle Ages 18-19
mints 30
mint marks 23, 30
mohur 44
money changers 19
Muhammad 24
Muslims 24-25, 26

names 34
national symbols 34

oban 23
owl coins 15

Palmstruch, Johann 8-9
penny 27, 30, 34, 45
pieces of eight 39
plastic cards 11
pound 34, 36
Ptolemies 26

quadrans 17

rarest coins 45
Renaissance 20-21
Roman coins 5, 13, 16-17, 26, 31, 33, 34, 42
Romulus and Remus 16

salt 10
Saladin 25
Santa Cruz 10
semis 17
sestertius 17
Shepton Mallet 33
shells 6, 38
shillings 27, 38
Silbannacus 31
silver 7, 12, 13, 21, 28,36
smallest 44
smart cards 11
stone money 10
South Africa 8
South America 28
strata 32
striking coins 6-7
Sutton Hoo 41
Sweden 5, 9

testing 36
testoon 20, 21

thaler 21
tobacco leaves 29
'touching' 40
trade 33, 14
treasure 19, 39
Turkey 6, 35

United States of America 28-29, 34

Vigo Bay 31
Vikings 19, 28

wampum 28-29
War of Independence 29
watermarks 35, 37
wealthiest person 45
wishing wells 41

Yap stones 10

Zeus 14

FURTHER READING

Cribb, J., Eyewitness Guides: *Money*, Dorling Kindersley, 1991.

Mackay, J., *The Beginner's Guide to Coin Collecting*, Apple Press, 1991.

Krause, L. and Mishler, C., *Standard Catalog of World Coins*, Krause Publications, frequent new editions.

Pick, A., *Standard Catalogue of World Paper Money*, Krause Publications, frequent new editions.

Ralph Lewis, B., *Coins and Currency*, Reed International, 1993.

Seaby, H. and Seaby, P., *Standard Catalogue of British Coins*, Seaby, published annually.